Where Is
North Carolina?

W0114253

Where Is
North Carolina?

by Tracy Vonder Brink

illustrated by Ted Hammond

Penguin Workshop

For my friend who found happiness in
North Carolina's mountains—TVB

PENGUIN WORKSHOP
An imprint of Penguin Random House LLC
1745 Broadway, New York, NY 10019
penguinrandomhouse.com

Copyright © 2026 by Penguin Random House LLC

Penguin Random House values and supports copyright. Copyright fuels creativity,
encourages diverse voices, promotes free speech, and creates a vibrant culture. Thank you
for buying an authorized edition of this book and for complying with copyright laws by not
reproducing, scanning, or distributing any part of it in any form without permission. You
are supporting writers and allowing Penguin Random House to continue to publish books
for every reader. Please note that no part of this book may be used or reproduced in any
manner for the purpose of training artificial intelligence technologies or systems.

PENGUIN is a registered trademark and PENGUIN WORKSHOP is a trademark
of Penguin Books Ltd. WHO HQ & Design is a registered trademark of
Penguin Random House LLC.

Designed and Produced by Dinardo Design, LLC.

Library of Congress Cataloging-in-Publication Data is available.

First published in the United States of America by Penguin Workshop, 2026

Manufactured in the United States of America
CJKW

ISBN 9798217053254 (paperback)
10 9 8 7 6 5 4 3 2 1

ISBN 9798217053261 (library binding)
10 9 8 7 6 5 4 3 2 1

The authorized representative in the EU for product safety and compliance is
Penguin Random House Ireland, Morrison Chambers, 32 Nassau Street,
Dublin D02 YH68, Ireland, https://eu-contact.penguin.ie.

Contents

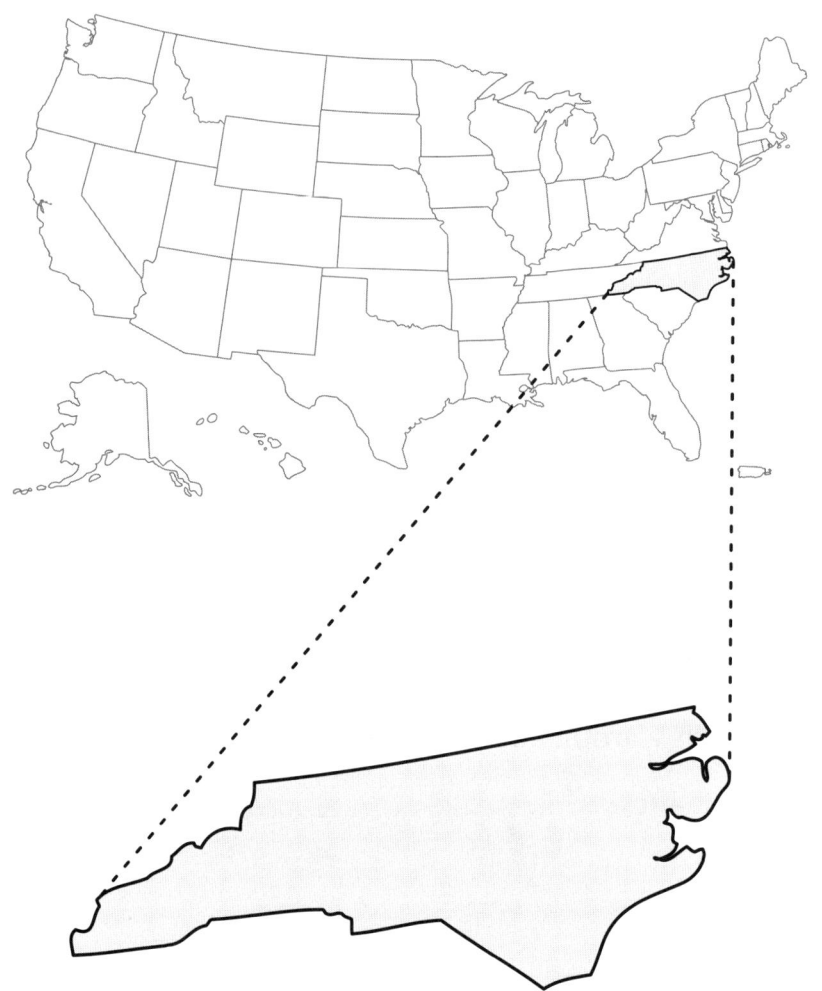

Where Is North Carolina?

Of all the pirates to hunt the seas, Blackbeard was one of the most feared. He wore a tall fur hat and strapped six pistols to his chest. He lit matches and stuck them in his bushy beard so the smoke circled his face. The ship he sailed on was called the *Queen Anne's Revenge*. It flew black flags, perhaps with skulls and crossbones on them.

Blackbeard's real name may have been Edward Teach, but nobody knows for sure. Little is known of his early life. We do know he helped the English capture ships during Queen Anne's War between 1702 and 1713 and became a pirate after that. By the fall of 1717, Blackbeard was raiding ships in the Atlantic Ocean around the Caribbean Islands. He had more than three hundred pirates under his command!

In 1718, Blackbeard and his pirates tried to sail their ships into an inlet (a narrow strip of water leading to the sea) on the North Carolina shore. The water wasn't deep enough, and their ships got stuck. Some said Blackbeard ran aground on purpose to get rid of the ships and to split off from some of the pirates. He and a group of around thirty pirates abandoned the rest of the crew and took off with the loot. Legend says Blackbeard buried his treasure somewhere in the Outer Banks. None of it has ever been found.

People who live along North Carolina's coast and visitors to the state have never stopped looking for it.

CHAPTER 1
Welcome to North Carolina

North Carolina's deep roots stretch back to its earliest people and the settlers who made it a state. The Tar Heel State is a modern state, too—its cities welcome new companies and businesses. North Carolina also has beautiful mountains and sandy beaches. No wonder it's one of the fastest-growing states in the country!

North Carolina's total land area is 48,624 square miles, making it the twenty-ninth largest US state. At 560 miles wide, North Carolina is the widest state east of the Mississippi River. The Atlantic Ocean forms its eastern border, and Tennessee lies to its west. Virginia is to its north. Georgia and South Carolina sit to the south.

The state has three main regions. The Coastal

Plain is low, flat land in the east. This area covers about 45 percent of the state and includes the Outer Banks, a chain of barrier islands (long, narrow islands parallel to a coast). The Piedmont (say: PEED-mont) sits in the middle and takes up about 45 percent of North Carolina. This high, flat area stretches between the Coastal Plain and the Mountains. The Mountains in the west make

up the third region. The Black Mountains, Blue Ridge Mountains, and Great Smoky Mountains are all found there. They're part of the larger system of Appalachian Mountains, one of the oldest mountain ranges in the United States. Mount Mitchell, the tallest peak east of the Mississippi River, is located here. It's 6,684 feet above sea level!

Traces of the first people to live in what is now North Carolina have been found in the Piedmont. About ten thousand years ago, Indigenous people took stone from the mountains and used it to make tools and spear tips. We don't know what these people called themselves, but they were probably made up of many nations. One of the places where they dug and crafted stone is now known as the Hardaway Site, named after a construction company that was working on the land where the artifacts (objects made by ancient people) were discovered. More than one million Indigenous artifacts have been found there!

The descendants of these first Indigenous peoples spread throughout what is now North Carolina. Their languages all belonged to the Algonquian (say: al-GON-kwee-uhn) language family. Later, their descendants formed the Catawba, Cherokee, Creek, and many other nations. By the time the first European settlers arrived in the 1500s, about thirty Indigenous nations made their homes in North Carolina.

The English were the first non-Indigenous people to settle there. In 1587, they built a colony on Roanoke Island, off the coast. That same year, a baby named Virginia Dare was born. She was the first English baby born in the American colonies. Three years later, her grandfather sailed from England to bring supplies to Roanoke. When he arrived, he found it empty! The only clue left behind was the word CROATOAN carved into a wooden post. Some think it meant the colonists had moved to nearby Croatoan Island to join the Indigenous people who lived there, but nobody knows for sure.

In 1663, England's King Charles II created a new province (a district or region) south of Virginia, even though Indigenous people already lived there. He called it Carolina, from the Latin word for his own name. Settlers in Carolina were allowed to attend any Christian church they wanted—something they couldn't do in many European countries. People from England, Germany, and Switzerland flocked to the new province. Some forced enslaved African people to come with them to work on farms and as servants in homes for no pay.

In 1705, European settlers founded the first town in what would become North Carolina. They

named it Bath, after an English city. Blackbeard came to Bath several years later and promised the English government that he'd stop being a pirate. He anchored a ship, the *Adventure*, in waters near Ocracoke Island. Blackbeard didn't keep his promise and returned to being a pirate. The coastal colonies wanted him stopped. Two Royal Navy ships cornered the *Adventure* in an inlet in the Outer Banks. Blackbeard was killed. The inlet

where he died became known as Teach's Hole.

In 1712, England split Carolina into North and South Carolina. At that time, life was hard in Scotland, the northern section of Great Britain (which also included England). Many there were poor. Land was cheaper to buy in the American colonies than in Scotland, so a group called the Scots-Irish moved to North Carolina in hopes of finding a better life. (They're called Scots-Irish because their Scottish ancestors had moved to Northern Ireland.) Starting in the 1740s, they settled in the Piedmont and in the Appalachian Mountains.

North Carolina had warm summers, mild winters, and plenty of rain, so crops could be grown for almost eight months a year. This attracted settlers from Virginia who moved south to farm. Soil in the Piedmont and the Coastal Plain was good for growing tobacco and cotton.

The Coastal Plain was also full of pine trees.

Their wood and sap were turned into tar, a sticky liquid used to waterproof ships, and turpentine, burned as fuel in lamps. Some settlers farmed their own land, but others enslaved people as workers. By 1767, about forty thousand enslaved African people had been forced to live in North Carolina.

In 1776, North Carolina was the first American colony to vote for independence from England. Six to seven thousand North Carolinians joined the fight. Some were sent to help George Washington's army in 1777. Others fought in North Carolina—five Revolutionary War battles took place there. After the United States won its independence, North Carolina became the twelfth state in 1789. That same year, the University of North Carolina in Chapel Hill became the first public university in the United States.

Ten years later, the state had the first gold

rush in the United States. A twelve-year-old boy found a seventeen-pound gold nugget in a creek on his family's land. Thousands began pouring into the Piedmont in search of gold. Until 1828, all the gold for the gold coins made by the US government came from the state.

These changes in the United States harmed North Carolina's Indigenous people. In the 1830s, the US government passed a law that made the people of the Cherokee, Choctaw, Chickasaw, Creek, and Seminole Nations leave their lands in the east and move west. US soldiers forced sixteen thousand Cherokee people from North Carolina, Tennessee, Georgia, and Alabama to march to Oklahoma. At least four thousand died during the trip. This forced march became known as the Trail of Tears.

Some Indigenous people found ways to stay in North Carolina. The Lumbee people lived in the southeastern wetlands in areas settlers couldn't farm, so they were able to remain on their land. Sixty families of the Cherokee Oconaluftee (say: oh-con-uh-LUF-tee) Citizen Indians had agreements with the North Carolina government that allowed them to stay. About four hundred Cherokee hid in the mountains. Others who survived the Trail of Tears later made their way back. The descendants of these groups became the Eastern Band of the Cherokee.

CHAPTER 2
The Rip Van Winkle State

North Carolina seemed to grow so slowly in the early 1800s that it was called the Rip Van Winkle State, after the fairy tale character who slept for years. The state's leaders at that time didn't believe that its government should spend money to improve schools, roads, or farms. Between 1815 and 1840, hundreds of thousands of North Carolinians moved out of the state to find better jobs.

In 1860, the United States was torn between those who wanted to ban slavery and those who wanted to keep it. At that time, more than three hundred thousand enslaved Black people lived in North Carolina. Over half of white North Carolinians were never enslavers, but of those who were, many controlled North Carolina's government and businesses.

Abraham Lincoln felt slavery was wrong and spoke out against it when he ran for president. When he was elected, the Southern states didn't want a president who was anti-slavery, so they left the United States to form their own country. They called themselves the Confederate States of America, or the Confederacy. The US government fought to make these states stay, and the Civil War began on April 12, 1861. A month later, North Carolina left the United States and joined the Confederacy.

The Civil War gave North Carolina one of its nicknames. In an 1863 battle, troops from North Carolina stood their ground and fought when other Confederate soldiers ran. The North Carolinians joked that the other soldiers should put North Carolina tar on their heels to help them "stick better in the next fight." After another battle, a general said the North Carolina "tar heels" had done well, and the name stuck. Later, when the University of North Carolina's sports teams needed a nickname, they called themselves the Tar Heels. This is still the university's mascot today.

During the Civil War, 130,000 North Carolinians fought for the Confederacy. About eight thousand fought on the Union (the US government) side, including five thousand Black North Carolinians. The state became a battleground as the Union and Confederacy fought to control its coast where ships full of supplies could land. The Battle of Bentonville was the largest to happen in the state—eighty thousand soldiers fought there. By the end of the war, over forty thousand North Carolinians had died in the fighting.

The Civil War ended in 1866. That same year, the North Carolina government agreed that the Eastern Band of the Cherokee could stay on fifty thousand acres of land, called the Qualla Boundary, which had been bought for them by William Holland Thomas. (At this time, the law said Indigenous people could not buy or own land.) He was a white man who had been adopted into the Cherokee community. Two years later, the US government recognized the Eastern Band of the Cherokee as a sovereign nation (a nation with its own government).

North Carolina rejoined the United States in 1868. Its new state constitution gave Black men the right to vote. It also said that all children in the state had the right to go to public school. The US government set up the Freedmen's

BIG COVE

WOLF TOWN

YELLOW HILL

BIRD TOWN   PAINT TOWN

The Qualla Boundary in the late 1800s

Bureau to help people who had formerly been enslaved build schools. Black communities in the state also raised money to pay for school buildings and teachers. Some white people didn't want Black children to be educated. The Ku Klux Klan, a white supremacist hate group, threatened teachers and attacked Black people.

Times were hard. Many Black people had their freedom but not much else. Often, poor white people also couldn't afford their own land. Poor Black and white people had no choice but to rent farmland that had once been worked by enslaved people. Instead of paying money for the land, they shared their crops with the landowners. This way of farming, called sharecropping, made it hard for farmers to have enough crops left over to sell. It kept many poor. By 1880, these kinds of rental lands made up one-third of North Carolina's farms.

Before the Civil War, North Carolina factories

turned cotton into cloth and yarn. In the late 1800s, businessmen in North Carolina built more of these factories, called textile mills. (A textile is woven or knitted cloth.) At the same time, the difficulties of sharecropping sent North Carolinians looking for other kinds of work. People left farms to take jobs in the mills. Textiles

became a booming business. Edwin Holt's textile mills in Alamance County made colorful cotton fabrics, and Alamance Plaid became a bestseller. Cannon Mills opened in Concord and wove the first towels made in the South. By the mid-1890s, North Carolina had 182 cotton mills and ten mills for woolen goods.

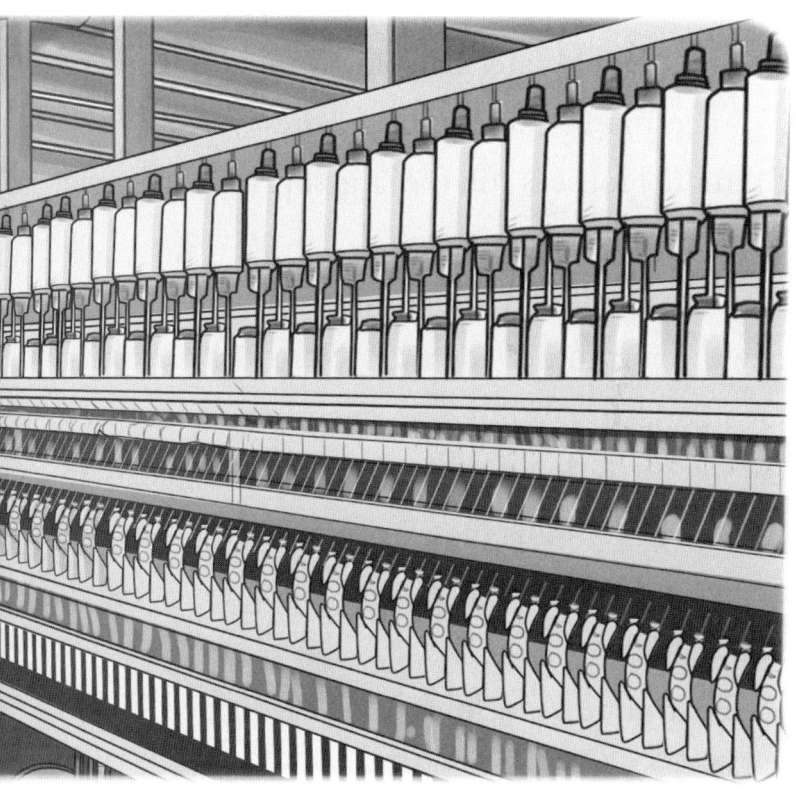

Times weren't hard for everyone. One of North Carolina's most famous places opened in 1895. George Washington Vanderbilt, a member of one of America's richest families, built a country home near Asheville. Called the Biltmore House, it covered more than four acres and had 250 rooms—including 43 bathrooms! The grounds covered 125,000 acres of land. (Some of the land would later be sold to the government and became Pisgah National Forest.) Today, the Biltmore House is still the largest privately owned home in the United States.

The end of the nineteenth century brought new opportunities to some North Carolinians. George Henry White was one of the first Black lawyers in North Carolina and served terms in the North Carolina House of Representatives and Senate. Voters elected him to Congress in 1896 and 1898.

That same year, John Merrick opened North

Carolina Mutual Life, a company that sold insurance (money paid to help with accidents, fires, and sickness) to Black people. Merrick had been born enslaved and became a successful businessman. At that time, Black people weren't allowed to use the same businesses or schools as white people. This is called segregation. Because Black customers weren't welcome at most white-owned businesses, Merrick also helped found the first bank, hospital, drug store, and public library for Black North Carolinians.

If North Carolina really was the Rip Van Winkle State, then it was about to wake up.

CHAPTER 3
On the Move

North Carolina grew and changed in the twentieth century. Hundreds of textile and tobacco mills turned the state's cotton and tobacco into goods to be sold in northern and southern cities. North Carolina forests provided wood that became furniture in the state's forty-four furniture factories. In Thomasville, the Standard Chair Company manufactured rocking chairs for Sears, Roebuck and Company. Based in Chicago, it was one of the largest sellers of goods in the country.

Furniture salesmen in North Carolina realized companies from all over America liked their products. They started the High Point Furniture Market so that buyers could come and shop. The market would go on to be held twice a year for more than one hundred years. It's still held today!

In 1910, the president of Sears, Roebuck and Company, Julius Rosenwald, wanted to help improve rural southern schools for Black students. He partnered with educator Booker T. Washington to match money raised by local communities to build or improve Black schools. North Carolina built eight hundred Rosenwald schools, more than any other state.

An invention that was a bit more complicated than a chair took off in North Carolina. In 1900, brothers Orville and Wilbur Wright were looking for a place to test a new flying machine. They needed somewhere with strong winds and open spaces to take off and land. The beaches of Kitty Hawk, a small fishing village on the Outer Banks, seemed perfect. The wind blew steadily there, and the sand would make a soft landing place. The brothers visited Kitty Hawk and tested

some gliders (planes that fly without engines). Then, they went home to Ohio to work on their invention.

In 1903, the Wright brothers returned to Kitty Hawk to try out their new machine. They called it the *Flyer*. It was powered by an engine they'd built. On December 13, Orville climbed in and took off. The *Flyer* was only in the air for twelve seconds, but it flew!

Around the time the Wright brothers were flying at Kitty Hawk, a North Carolinian named Bascom Lamar Lunsford started collecting mountain music. He'd grown up hearing his family sing and play songs handed down by the Scots-Irish immigrants who settled in North Carolina's mountains. This type of music, called folk music, was played on the fiddle and on the banjo, an instrument created by enslaved African people.

Lunsford visited mountain communities to learn folk music. He could play three hundred songs from memory and wrote down more than three thousand! Lunsford recorded songs for the Library of Congress and started the Mountain Dance and Folk Festival in Asheville. His work helped people around the world learn about folk music.

North Carolina was on the move in the 1920s. The state government passed a bill to build a state highway system and paved more than seven thousand miles of state roads. The road-building project helped North Carolina become known as the Good Roads State. Trucks used those roads to carry goods to market. Soon, North Carolina led the South in manufacturing (producing large quantities of goods in factories).

The government and people of North Carolina also gave money to the state's colleges—the University of North Carolina (UNC) and Duke University both added buildings to their campuses. One of college basketball's biggest rivalries began in 1920 as the two universities played each other for the first time. UNC beat Duke then and today leads the rivalry with 145 overall wins to Duke's 120.

In the late 1920s, people in North Carolina and Tennessee worried that companies were cutting down too many trees for wood. People in both states wanted to set aside part of the Great Smoky Mountains as a national park. The states' governments gave money to buy land for the park. Ordinary people raised funds, too—more than 4,500 kids saved pennies and donated over $1,000! By the 1930s, hundreds of thousands of acres in the mountains had been bought. It was divided evenly between North Carolina and Tennessee to make the park. Great Smoky Mountains National Park opened for the first time in 1940.

North Carolina began as a state that depended on textiles, furniture, and tobacco. In the 1950s, many college graduates left the state looking for other sorts of work. State leaders looked for ways to bring in new jobs. They thought that the research (careful study to find out more about something) being done at UNC-Chapel Hill, North Carolina State, and Duke University might attract new companies. The state set aside seven thousand acres between the three cities and created Research Triangle Park. It opened in 1959, and by the end of the year, five companies had moved there.

More change came to North Carolina in the 1950s. Black North Carolinians had worked for many years to end segregation and laws that made life harder for them. They wanted to be able to go to the same schools and shops as white people and to be treated fairly. After the US Supreme Court ruled that keeping Black students out of white schools was against the Constitution, Black students in North Carolina were finally able to attend white schools. Then, Black North Carolinians worked to end segregation in all public places across the state by staging protests and taking the state government to court.

The Greensboro Sit-in

Laws across the United States once kept Black people separated from white people. Black people weren't allowed to use the same stores, restaurants, bathrooms, or even drinking fountains as white people.

In 1960, four Black college students, Ezell Blair Jr. (now Jibreel Khazan), David Richmond, Franklin McCain, and Joseph McNeil, decided to change that. They sat at a lunch counter at a store called Woolworth's in Greensboro and asked to be served. They were told to leave. The students stayed until the restaurant closed. The next day, they came back with more students from local colleges. By the fifth day, more than three hundred people filled the store to protest the segregated lunch counter.

When the same thing began happening at other Woolworth's stores around the country, the

company gave in. Six months after the Greensboro Four, as they became known, tried to order lunch, Black customers were being served at the Greensboro Woolworth's.

This kind of peaceful protest became known as a sit-in. Groups have used sit-ins to work to change unfair laws and rules ever since.

New jobs and fairer laws made more people stay in and move to North Carolina. Its population increased from four million to five million between 1950 and 1970. North Carolina had changed from a sleepy state to a place many wanted to live.

CHAPTER 4
The Great State of North Carolina

Today, North Carolina remains one of the country's fastest-growing states. More than eleven million people call it home. Charlotte is its biggest city and is the second-largest center for banks in the United States. Raleigh, its capital, is the second biggest city in the state. It's called the City of Oaks for the many tall oak trees that line its streets. Greensboro, Durham, and Winston-Salem are North Carolina's other large cities.

The state has the largest Indigenous population east of the Mississippi River. More than 130,000 Indigenous people live in North Carolina. The Eastern Band of the Cherokee still make their homes in the Qualla Boundary. The Lumbee are the largest nation in the state and live in the southeast along the banks of the Lumbee River. The Lumbee Tribe formed a school system that still operates today, alongside other Indigenous groups who work to strengthen education in their communities and North Carolina.

Farming continues to be an important part of North Carolina's economy and brings in more than $100 billion each year. Tar Heel farmers raise more turkeys and grow more sweet potatoes than any other state. The sweet potato is the official state vegetable! North Carolina also ranks in the top ten states for producing cucumbers, chickens, pigs, and tobacco. Apples are a growing business, too—North Carolina's apple orchards produce more than 150 million pounds of apples every year.

North Carolina continues to lead the nation in making textiles. HanesBrands, one of the country's largest producers of T-shirts, underwear, and more, has its headquarters in Winston-Salem.

The state is still known for its furniture and has the world's largest furniture store and the world's largest chest of drawers—thirty-six feet high!

Research Triangle Park has continued to grow and now houses more than 375 companies, including IBM and Cisco Systems, making it the largest research park in the United States. Scientists Gertrude Elion and George Hitchings won the Nobel Prize in Medicine for life-saving medicines they invented there. Its success has inspired other states to build their own research parks.

The state is known for its farms and businesses, but it's also loved for its natural beauty and outdoor fun. More than twelve million people have visited Great Smoky Mountains National Park every year since 2019, making it the most visited national park in the country. The Great Smoky Mountains are known as the Salamander Capital of the World because so many different kinds of salamanders live there, including the hellbender. Hellbenders may grow to be up to twenty-nine inches long! Hikers also enjoy more than 1,700 miles of trails in the state's four national forests. Every year, more than a quarter million hikers climb to the top of Chimney Rock to take in the view from 2,280 feet above the valley floor.

Cape Hatteras lighthouse, built in 1870

People also have fun on the sandy beaches of the Outer Banks and Cape Hatteras National Seashore. The national seashore includes more than seventy miles of beach. Sea turtles and seals can be spotted there. Wild horses roam free in parts of the Outer Banks, too.

Visitors can follow in Blackbeard's footsteps on Ocracoke Island. They can also see artifacts from his ship at the North Carolina Maritime

Museum in Beaufort and the Graveyard of the Atlantic Museum in Hatteras and learn more about the history of the thousands of ships that wrecked off North Carolina's dangerous shore.

A small coastal fishing town created a unique way to cook seafood. The catch of the day—especially shrimp—was lightly dusted in corn flour or corn meal and deep fried on the docks of Calabash starting in the 1930s. It became known as Calabash-style and was soon popular outside of the state. North Carolinians also have their own way of doing barbecue, brushing pork with spices and vinegar as it cooks.

Asheville's Mountain Dance and Folk Festival, started by Bascom Lamar Lunsford, still happens every year. It's been held for more years than any other folk music festival in the United States. North Carolina is known for folk music, but other important musicians also lived there. Walker Calhoun, an elder of the Eastern Band of the Cherokee, played and taught traditional Cherokee music for more than sixty years. Jazz greats Nina Simone and John Coltrane were both North Carolinians. Simone's childhood home in Tryon became a historic site in 2018. Visitors to Tryon can also see a mural painted in her honor. The John Coltrane International Jazz and Blues Festival is held in his hometown of High Point.

Along with the great outdoors and music,

North Carolinians love sports. Michael Jordan's family moved to Wilmington when he was five. He played basketball at the University of North Carolina for three years before going pro. Later, he owned the Charlotte Hornets, the state's National Basketball Association team, for thirteen years. The Carolina Panthers are also based in Charlotte. They've been the state's National Football League team since 1995. Racecar legend Junior Johnson grew up as part of a farm family in the foothills and went on to win fifty of NASCAR's top races.

North Carolinians and visitors enjoy the state's warm summers and mild winters, but its coast makes it vulnerable to hurricanes. Since 1851, more than forty hurricanes have made direct hits on the state. In 2024, Hurricane Helene devastated western North Carolina. Floods, high winds, and tornadoes damaged or destroyed more than 250,000 homes and killed over a hundred people. Popular destinations like Chimney Rock and Lake Lure were also damaged. North Carolina–based companies pledged millions of dollars to help people rebuild and recover.

North Carolina was one of the original thirteen colonies, but it's no longer the sleepy state of the past. It's home to some of the top researchers and companies in the country. Its people celebrate their culture and traditions and love North Carolina's natural beauty. North Carolinians past and present have left their mark on their state. They make it what it is today.

North Carolina at a Glance

Statehood: 1789

Nickname: The Tar Heel State

Abbreviation: NC

State Motto: *Esse quam videri* (Latin for "To be rather than to seem")

State Tree: Pine

State Animal: Gray squirrel

Capital: Raleigh

Size: 53,819 square miles

Population: Over 11 million

Famous People from North Carolina:

MrBeast (YouTuber), Dale Earnhardt Sr. and Jr. (NASCAR drivers), Thelonius Monk (jazz musician), Dolley Madison (First Lady)

State flag

State bird
Cardinal

State flower
Flowering dogwood

FUN FACT:
Linville Gorge, in Pisgah National Forest, is called the Grand Canyon of the East because it goes two thousand feet deep!

Timeline of North Carolina

10,000 BCE	Indigenous people make stone tools and spear points at the Hardaway Site
1712	Carolina is divided into North Carolina and South Carolina
1789	North Carolina becomes the twelfth US state
1866	Eastern Band of the Cherokee wins the right to stay on their land in the Qualla Boundary
1868	North Carolina rejoins the United States following the Civil War
1898	John Merrick founds North Carolina Mutual Life
1903	The Wright brothers make their first successful flight at Kitty Hawk
1940	Great Smoky Mountains National Park opens
1960	Black college students hold sit-in protests at Woolworths in Greensboro
1981	Michael Jordan plays his first game for the University of North Carolina
2018	Jazz singer Nina Simone's home becomes a historic site
2024	Hurricane Helene hits North Carolina

Timeline of the World

9000 BCE	The city of Jericho is built in what is now Palestine
1713	England and France agree to end Queen Anne's War
1789	George Washington inaugurated as the first US president
1866	The first underwater cable to send messages is laid between Ireland and Newfoundland
1869	Suez Canal opens in Egypt, linking the Mediterranean and Red Seas
1898	Spain declares war on the United States, starting the Spanish-American War
1903	The Tour de France, a three-week bicycle race, is held for the first time
1939	World War II begins
1957	The Soviet Union launches Sputnik, the world's first satellite
1981	England's Prince Charles and Lady Diana Spencer are engaged
2005	YouTube is launched
2019	Chinese spacecraft becomes the first to touch down on the far side of the moon
2024	The thirty-third Olympic Games are held in Paris

Bibliography

*Books for young readers

*Berne, Emma Carlson. ***What Do We Know About the Lost Colony of Roanoke?*** New York: Penguin Workshop, 2025.

*Buckley, James, Jr. ***Who Was Blackbeard?*** New York: Penguin Workshop, 2015.

*Buckley, James, Jr. ***Who Were the Wright Brothers***? New York: Penguin Workshop, 2014.

*Edwards, Doris. ***North Carolina***. North Mankato: Abdo Publishing, 2023.

*Sommer, Nathan. ***North Carolina***. Minnetonka: Bellwether Media, 2022.

Websites

Kids National Geographic:

kids.nationalgeographic.com/geography/states/article/north-carolina

North Carolina Secretary of State's Office:

sosnc.gov/divisions/publications/kids_page_famous

sosnc.gov/divisions/publications/kids_page_cities

sosnc.gov/divisions/publications/kids_page_geography

sosnc.gov/divisions/publications/kids_page_history